For Leslie
with thanks for
your interest ~

Lee

By the same author:


**IN VITRO: New Short Rhyming Poems Post-9/11 (2009)**

"At his best, Jamieson resembles a modern-day G.M. Hopkins" —
*Kirkus Discoveries.*
"Splendid gem... Striking language that suddenly becomes
metaphysical and intricate" —
*Bonzer.*
"Vivid landscape... rhyme... packed with detail" —
*Wild Violet.*


**21ST CENTURY BREAD: Short Rhyming Poems Post-9/11 (2007)**

"Musical... ripe with verbs... a clear voice... snappy enjambed lines
given to the playfulness of rhyme" —
*Centrifugal Eye.*
"Calls to be read out loud... consonants play off each other
from the very first lines" —
*The Non-Euclidian Café.*
"A volume of unusual unity and grace... line
by line... an outstanding book" —
*Contemporary Rhyme.*

# HOW TO RHYME YOUR WAY TO 'METAPHOR POEMS'

## FOR POETS-TO-BE & TEACHERS-TO-BE

LELAND JAMIESON

By the same author:
*IN VITRO: NEW SHORT RHYMING POEMS POST-9/11*
Copyright © 2009
Available direct from the printer
at www.createspace.com/3372169
or your favorite bookseller
or Amazon.com.

*21ST CENTURY BREAD: SHORT RHYMING POEMS POST-9/11*
Copyright © 2007
Available direct from the printer
at www.createspace.com/3371994
or your favorite bookseller
or Amazon.com.

*HOW TO RHYME YOUR WAY TO 'METAPHOR POEMS':*
*FOR POETS-TO-BE & TEACHERS-TO-BE*
Copyright © 2012 by Leland Jamieson

ISBN-13: 978-1470040581
ISBN-10: 1470040581

Printed in the U.S.A.
Cover design by CreateSpace.
Front cover photo © António Jorge Da Silva Nunes/Dreamtime.com.
Back cover photo © G.K. Jamieson.
Available direct from the printer
at www.createspace.com/3792613
or your favorite bookseller
or Amazon.com.

# CONTENTS

# 1. A Personal Welcome to Poets-to-Be & Teachers-to-Be

Do you like, or *would* you like, to express yourself and your feelings in a poem which does not later embarrass you?

Would you like to go more deeply and with more perception in a poem than you seem able to do at this time in your life?

And would you like to compose poetry *more easily* than you are able to now, if that were possible without compromising a poem's honesty and quality?

Do you think you may, possibly, want to teach English at the high school or college level, but you wonder whether you could handle the poetry instruction?

If you answered "yes" to any of these questions, read on. This book is for you.

From my early teens I consciously wanted to write poems that rhymed. Try as I might, they were awful — forced rhymes made them ridiculous. I gave up finally and joined the free verse poets. I was afraid I'd never acquire the ability to think up unforced end-rhymes.

I chose William Carlos Williams as my mentor. I read and studied all his poetry, as well as a big biography, and, in it, much of the correspondence between him and both Ezra Pound and T.S. Eliot.

Williams had a deep longing to discover a metrical system to replace the English Foot. Yet this eluded him all his life. He had been a strong voice leading us out of the 19th Century's clichéd sentiment, language, and subject matter. His voice, among others, ended the overly-stressed ta-TUM ta-TUM ta-TUM that characterized most public readings of English and American Poetry of that time. We can thank him for that.

Even in the hands of his followers, however, his "revolution" has failed to this day to solve "the problem of rhythm" in free verse. (I address some of the inherent reasons why in Chapter 7.)

My own free verse poems, even the 39 or so that found publishers, were more than a disappointment to me. In hindsight, they probably never deserved publication.

I set out, at last, to learn how to write metrical or "blank" verse on contemporary themes. That mastered to a small degree, I turned again to an effort to learn how to write unforced end-rhymes. I finally stumbled, yes, literally *stumbled,* upon an approach which made natural-sounding end-rhymes possible, even easy, for me to write.

*The result was a liberation of my imagination, feeling, and consciousness to a degree I had never before experienced!*

This little book can make it possible for you, too, more easily to write natural-sounding end-rhymes. And it can liberate your imagination, feeling, and consciousness as well.

### How I Stumbled on Random-Potential "Reverse" Rhyming

Rhymes are slight and silly little things to be afraid of — but for most of my life I *was* afraid of them. As I've said, I was afraid I couldn't find a rhyming word to express what I wanted to say that would not distort the meaning intended. And I was equally afraid to manipulate lines into metrical rhythm because it made them sound sing-song when read. Both were writer's (poet's) blocks for me. (Maybe they are for you, too!)

I stumbled upon a strategy for how to use a rhyming dictionary that I imagine is somewhat akin to random-potential "probability theory" in modern physics. After composing the first *metrical* line of a new poem, I opened my rhyming dictionary. I scanned a list of rhymes matching the end-word of my first line. Working at random, but also by intuition, and responding to the suggestiveness of each of the rhyme words, *I let one of them — possessing nothing but pure potential — draw out of my heart and mind the most appropriate next line's imagery, action, feeling, or thought.* You might call it "reverse composition." I call it "Reverse Rhyming."

(This was a big change from my usual mode of composing. That was to expect, once I was already in and even near the end of the next line, to struggle to come up with a rhyme word to end it so it made sense and felt and sounded right. It never did.)

Let me state this as clearly as I can: The process is "reverse" because *rather than starting a new line and struggling for a rhyme,* ***you start with the rhyme and let it gently pull the new line into place without too strict a preconception of what that line might say.***

(This is not to be confused with another use of the term, "reverse rhyming," which is to make the *initial word* of each line rhyme. We have no interest in that in this book.)

Let me repeat, in different words: *First find the rhyme, and only then the new line. Do this without too strict a preconception of what the new line might say, or what words it might employ.* I don't want to press this dynamic to the point of surrealism or

10

deconstructionist chaos. I only want to impress upon you this: Be open to the possibility that the poem may take you *coherently* to a new and different place than you imagined when you first set out to compose. Be alert to this, and go with it. *Your creativity lies within the poem, not apart from it or outside it, not even apart from it somewhere in your heart or head.*

In addition, I learned to manipulate meter with enjambment in a way that leads to a more natural reading, and *frees it from seduction by ta-TUMs*. It allows speech-stress more freedom to play its jazz-like counterpoint to the metrical and musical stresses of the line. This works especially well when the upper enjambed line's last word is an active verb that turns the reader without a pause to the next line below it. The absence of punctuation at the turning supports that reading.

I credit Reverse Rhyming and Enjambment with blasting open a dam which had held back my range of feeling and imagination. That is to say, it released an open and free-flowing river of creativity. Nothing I ever did (as I said, I'd been scribbling free verse since I was a teen) had ever opened up such a large, warm and exciting access to memory. Nothing I'd tried ever presented such serendipitous gifts of present-time awareness, sensitivity, perceptivity, and access to appropriate imagery. How could this be?

In my experience, free verse is less freeing in the making than formal verse because it tends to keep you in your left hemisphere, looking there, and from there outside, for inspiration.

A more *freeing* poetry, for me, and probably for you, is metrically manipulated rhyming (musical) lines. Working out the challenges inherent in crafting poems in such a *musical* manner *does* move one's thought processes to a large extent into the "feeling" right hemisphere (to be discussed in detail in Chapter 7). It is full of present-time awareness as well as memory, warmth of feeling, insights, delights, playfulness and surprises far superior to what the always-analytical left hemisphere can offer. (There's still plenty of use for "the left" when it comes time to make critical revisions.)

Let me invite you to anticipate the direct benefits to you of a *strategic* application of Reverse Rhyming. These will become apparent as you progress through this book:

1. A reverse rhyming poem starts with a *metrical* line describing *anything* which causes you, the poet, to feel warmth. The subject or topic (what the *poem* is "about") emerges only *later* in the process. This approach eliminates the crisis which you often

experience (and may express in moans and groans) when deciding what to write a poem "about." In fact, a rhyme word that particularly delights you with its warmth may cause you to change direction regarding what the poem is all about. It keeps you fluid and enables you to follow where the emerging coherence in the poem "wants to go," as you will see demonstrated when you reach chapters 3 and 4.

2. Reverse Rhyming is crucial to freeing you from the panic of not being able to find an appropriate unforced rhyme once past the first line of the poem.

3. The process helps you know how to handle matters when you are "stuck." Just try a new approach with a different line. Or try a different rhyme (to a new end word in the prior line synonymous with, or superior to, the original) to pull a new line into place.

4. Working in reverse rhyme builds vocabulary and reduces the temptation to fall back on clichés while you are selecting optimum rhymes from a larger universe than those that come first to mind.

5. Reverse rhyming offers a more supportive structure than free verse. That's because it focuses and stimulates and (believe it or not) *frees* you to be more creative in the process of thinking in similes and, subsequently, metaphors. This also helps you revise a poem with greater point and intelligence by offering a more artistically complex and *focused challenge* than free verse.

Would you, my good reader, like to take the same steps to move your poetry composition more deeply into the right hemisphere, and enjoy the same benefits?

If you are a poet-to-be, this little book is for you. If you are a teacher-to-be of English composition and literature (even if poetry is not your central interest in teaching) this is for you as well. In any case, if you are not sure, this is for you, too. It will help you *feel* sure, and secure, in your decision about how to move your career forward.

I believe this little volume will furnish both of you with an approach that will accelerate your learning this strategic process. You may fear you have nothing at all to say worth saying. *Yet, you will feel aroused by the music and rhythm which metrical reverse rhyming makes. You will discover you do have "something to say" — or the Muse does, through you.* The Muse speaks most originally through self-taught "meter-&-music-making" poets who write with their lips, fingers and ears.

And if you become a teacher, this book will give you a winning strategy for facing and drawing out students who feel resistant to poetry and express it in the classroom. How so? Because you will be accepting them as individuals with all their resistance and skepticism. You will be coaching that skepticism into something creative neither you nor they could possibly have imagined beforehand. (You'll find much more on this in Chapter 4.)

Surprise yourself! Discover that it is easier to write formal verse *well* than "free" verse *well*. Formal verse, framed in contemporary feeling that is yours, language that is yours, and images that are yours, is most truly freeing. Work that is *truly yours* will be contemporary and will deserve to be shared.

This book is an extensive re-write and expansion, by one fourth, of my 2009 volume, *Making 'Metaphor Poems' by Simile & Rhyme*. In that book I addressed the English teacher. I modeled the role he or she might play while coaching students to compose poetry out loud on their lips, fingers, and ears. In time, I came to realize that the book *also modeled the roles of students* in the process, though less obviously. That was because it did not speak to you directly, and in certain areas it failed to go into enough detail to be immediately helpful to you when working alone. This new title corrects those shortcomings and replaces the former book.

Here, then, is a new and enlarged book addressed to you, the individual student, who wants, perhaps, someday, to become a poet or English teacher. You may explore your desire alone, or in a small group. Chapters 3 and 4 are as simple, initially, as reading two pieces of short fiction. To make a deeper study of them, and to make their skills yours, just follow the instructions closely and respond to them interactively as modeled in the imaginary classroom. They should enable you, if you are motivated, easily to become self-taught on the topics taken up in this book.

Welcome to the poet's realm of metrical random-potential reverse rhyming, bursting with music and creativity that is almost magical!

# 2. How to Use This Book for Best Results

Read the book through in its entirety to grasp the overall picture before turning to a closer study to master any of the details. Except for chapters 3 and 4, the focus in this book is on the poet-to-be. However, you as a poet may well end up employed as a teacher to support yourself. Or, you may someday teach in poetry workshops. Absorb all the ideas you can from the teacher as modeled.

Next, jump in if you like wherever you are attracted and re-read what most excites you. Mark the book up as you go to make it your own (assuming it is your personal copy).

But if, like most of us, you are a "hands-on person" — a "*do it first* to get my head around it person" — you'll want to start your closer study with Chapter 3, doing the exercises just as the teacher (and your "7 Write-downs") instruct, to get the "whats" and "hows" in your hands and mind. Next, do the exercises in Chapter 4. Then study the other chapters to understand more fully the "whys." This works best for most people.

When you come to the line in Chapter 3 where the text instructs the teacher, **Put up on the blackboard or whiteboard the ta-TUMs,** *you* write them, and later, the lines that come beneath them, on sheets of paper as though they were "the board" on the wall. What you write will go in your notebook. I'll add more details later.

Let me explain some key terminology that deserves your attention. I have chosen the title to suggest the interplay of elements. Each contributes to your creativity:

**Rhyme:** In this approach to making poetry, the **verb** *Rhyme* is *the action avenue and generator of every line (except the first) in every stanza (or strophe) in all your poetic composition.* The **noun** *Rhyme* is the end word that matches the sound of other end words according to the scheme you have chosen. Our scheme, for simplicity, is the couplet, expressed AA, BB, CC... etc. **Reverse Rhyming** is defined in Chapter 1, and it is also defined by the major benefits it brings to you as a composer of poems. Those are also outlined there.

**Your Way:** There is a certain body of knowledge everyone has to learn, and to write *prose* about, if one is to become an educated grownup capable of earning a living and contributing to society. *The poetry that you compose is not a part of this body of knowledge. Poetry is not prose. Prose is not poetry, even when it has broken lines.*

Poetry springs from a place that is deepest in you which you may not know a whole lot about yet if you are a young poet-to-be. If you feel resistance to composing a poem dealing with a specific subject, this should sound an alert. It is quite possible that you are asking yourself to write about a topic you are not yet sufficiently acquainted with to be able to explore it fully, freely, and creatively.

Also, to write freely and compose from the heart, you need a certain ruthless honesty about the chatter in your head and what you feel in your heart. If you suspect that an idea, thought, or feeling is borrowed, is a cliché, is false, or might be a downright lie, it probably is. Above all, try to be truly honest with your feelings.

To take a particularly difficult example, perhaps you as a child lost a parent or sibling in circumstances (such as war) which prevented you from fully grieving your loss. You will probably have to do that grieving before you can write with depth and understanding about any aspect of that experience. (You may grieve as you compose, as I happened to do. In such a case, weep, and be grateful for the tears and the sense of relief that have finally come to you through composing poetry.) Revise and revise. Have patience with yourself as you move forward. Thus *your way* is an avenue that is unique to you. Every poet has his or her own.

**'Metaphor Poems':** I have put single quotes around this term in the title because there are few engaging poems that do *not* utilize metaphors. It is really a redundant expression. However, 'metaphor poem' is a key search term on the Internet. It's what teachers assign their students to encourage them to make their poetry reach into deeper levels of meaning than their first attempts. As a search term, it reflects students' needs to see clear examples so they can learn to employ metaphors. This little book attempts, also, to address those needs. In subsequent chapters I will both demonstrate the "metaphor" at greater length, and define it with respect to "simile," as well as supply a raft of illustrations.

**"Poem," "poetry"** and **"poet."** These share Greek and Sanscrit roots which mean "to make," "to gather," "to heap up." Making poetry is a radically different mental process compared to writing the theme, book review, or term paper most students find to be an all-too familiar and often exhausting process. In contrast, composing poetry by reverse rhyming is highly energizing for most poets-to-be.

**Stanza:** A stanza (or strophe) in poetry is the rough equivalent of a paragraph in prose. But whereas in prose you can manipulate and revise each paragraph solely with a view to its verbal content alone, in a formal poem each stanza will most usually have the same recurring pattern with respect both to the number of its metrical lines and its rhyme scheme, and you must allow for these as well.

You will not find in this little book a chapter devoted to working definitions or illustrations of three terms frequently found in discussions of poetry. They *are* important to the ear: 1) alliteration, 2) assonance, and 3) consonance. These are vital to the music-making of the *polished* poem. However, these musical elements are *not "auditory rhythmic drivers"* like end-rhymes and metrical rhythm (see Chapter 7). For the sake of brevity, I will leave it to you, the student, to discover them in your dictionary and apply them to your work when you are ready to move beyond the basics presented here.

I hope you poets-to-be and teachers-to-be will enjoy Reverse Rhyming. I don't imagine this is a new discovery. Though I'm far from the most well-read poet in the world, I have neither read of it anywhere, nor heard of it from others as a *strategic process in itself.* Of course, it is always an incidental tactic in formal poem-making. When I discovered it as a *strategic approach,* and put it to work systematically, as I've said, I found it immensely liberating of feeling, memory, and perception which had become blocked back when I was a child. I hope all poets-to-be will find it equally productive.

Regarding the choice of illustrative poems, I have selected 14 from my own first collection for several reasons. First, as a practical matter, I own the rights to them. Second, more important, they were all crafted with *true ear rhyme by the Reverse Rhyming strategy you will be practicing in the next chapter of this book.* Third, most poems exhibit metaphors in abundance. Fourth, they are reasonably contemporary in spirit. Fifth, they reflect subjects likely to be of at least some interest to students of both sexes. Sixth, they can be accessed by most young readers.

It's good advice to try to avoid underestimating a reader's intelligence or overestimating his or her knowledge, information, and experience. I hope I have struck a fair balance in this respect.

# 3.  Where and How to Start

**To the Poet-to-be:**

In this chapter and the next, I will be addressing the teacher. While I am busy at that, you will, in part, be busy gleaning what you can from the teacher's point of view.  Remember, you may someday want to teach.

However, the larger part of your goal is *to experience the process of reverse rhyming first-hand by doing as exercises all the things the teacher asks of the students in the imaginary classroom.* Remember, you will be writing your own poems, of your own choice of first lines, drawing on your own choice of words from the classroom's rhyme-sheets.  In other words, you will model your own *independent* work, step by step, on the work performed in the imaginary classroom in both this chapter and the next.

Specifically, on *separate sheets* of loose-leaf notebook paper you will write down at least the following as you prepare for, and subsequently compose, your own poems:

1) Your "ta-TUMs," and under them your own first "feeling line" ending in a one-syllable word with an "a," "e," "i," "o," or "u" vowel like those on the rhyme sheet lists.  Keep in mind the critical importance of being true to the language of *your own felt experience or perception.*  Avoid getting seduced by clichés and marketing lingo.

2) The rhyme words from each Rhyme Sheet in the text.

3) Your own trial lines (a set of three or more trials for each line of your poem).  From each set you will select one as your most workable new line to add to the poem.  Prepare these just as though you were a member of the class, speaking from lips to fingers, counting syllables (10) and stresses (5) into your ear, as illustrated in the text.

4) The poem you are composing, line by line, in rhyming couplets.  Go for 4-6 lines, at least, initially.

5) The steps you take to convert similes to metaphors. Model yours after the steps taken by the teacher.

6) The steps in your thinking that helped you arrive at a Constituting Metaphor for your title, and what you feel justifies it.

7) Any other notes you want to record.

Put these "7 Write-downs" in a three-ring binder in an

organized way for future reference. Use it to mark your progress as you write your own poems. Soon you will look back and be amazed, if you have applied yourself, at how far you have come in a short time.

**And Now to the Teacher-to-be:**

**Put up on the blackboard or whiteboard the ta-TUMs:**

ta-TUM    ta-TUM    ta-TUM    ta-TUM    ta-TUM

The point of the ta-TUMs is to get everyone dealing with real feelings in a rhythmic manner. It is easier to reach and sustain a feeling level with the rhythmic music of metrical rhymed poetry, for the reasons described in Chapter 7.

Here are four "openers" to get the process started. Four may be over-kill, but a good lesson plan should give you the security of several starts for backup. Or, you may simply have a preference for starting with one rather than another. If your schedule permits you to devote multiple sessions to poetry composition, this will give you several starters. You might begin with a question *and instructions:*

1) "How's everyone feeling today? Has this been a good day, or not?" If good, "What's made it a good day? Good *like* what? And *like* what else?" If a bad day, "Bad *like* what? And *like* what else?"

Let the initial round of responses subside, and then give them these instructions:

"I want you now to frame your answers in written lines ten syllables long, with five stresses to each line. Pattern them to match the ta-TUMs on the board, so that the *natural accents or naturally stressed syllables* fall beneath the *TUMs.* Write them out on scratch paper and count the syllables (10) and stresses (5) by quietly drumming your fingers on your desktops with one hand, while you whisper or murmur the line into the other hand cupped to your ear. Do this *before* you raise your hand to call it out.

"Again, the question is, 'How are you feeling? Is this a good day, or a bad day?' — what is it *like?*"

Give the students a few minutes to develop their responses while you list these instructional points in outline form on the board, or provide them by distributing handout sheets. It is important to communicate these instructions clearly so that the students' responses will be useful.

20

The *"likes"* will open up *similes*. By the end of this chapter and the next, you will be converting these to metaphors. But for now, put up to one side on the board all the students' responses.

When you have several five-stress statements with active verbs and nouns that will fit rhythmically under the ta-TUMs, discuss their strengths so students will understand the reasons for the choice you and they are about to make. Narrow the selection to offerings that end in a vowel other than a diphthong because these are especially rhyme-rich and unambiguous in how they sound. Further reduce this group to three. Select, with class participation, one of these, and write it up on the board under the ta-TUMs.

Next, tape up newsprint on the board for your first rhyme sheet and invite students to think up as many true ear-rhymes as they can, and proceed, from this point on, as modeled under "Rhyme Sheets."

Other starters, or for other days:

2.) "A time when you were really happy — what was it *like?*" Emphasize the instructions above about how they need to frame their responses before they raise their hands to be recognized.

3.) "Once when you were really sad — what was it *like?*" Emphasize the instructions above about how they need to frame their responses before they raise their hands to be recognized.

Another place to start is with feelings and attitudes about poetry itself.

4) "How many of you know how you truly feel about poetry? About making poems? About reading them? Let's take a vote. How many are uncertain how you really feel? Raise your hands.... How many know you *like* poetry? Raise your hands.... How many know you *don't?* Raise your hands please....

"Now, you can change your vote if you like...."

The point here is to encourage them to be honest with their feelings, because facing real feelings is the heart of poetry (in contrast to giving a socially-approved response, often in clichés). A first vote may be different from a second. The latter may reflect peer pressure when they see how others vote.

Chances are that one of these three lines will characterize the vote: "I 'like it' best tells you the way I feel"; "I 'hate it' best tells you the way I feel"; "I think I really don't know how I feel." Let's say, for example, the third line best matches the vote. Write it up under your ta-TUMs on the board:

```
ta  TUM  ta-TUM  ta  TUM  ta      TUM  ta  TUM
I   think  I   real  ly  don't  know  how   I     feel.
```

"This describe most of you? If not, give me another five-stress line that better describes what most of you feel about poetry."

(If you have a resistant student who blurts out a strongly negative feeling, in this step or an earlier one above, in opposition even to being involved in composing poetry, accept it and go directly into the strategy and tactics presented in Chapter 4.)

If the class is quiet, and offers no alternate student-generated line that can go beneath your ta-TUMs:

## Rhyme Sheets

"Okay, let's go with this line we have on the board. Now, everyone, give me every word you can think up that rhymes with *feel*."

Start a newsprint rhyme sheet (to be taped up and saved for future sessions): *feel.* List words they call out: *deal, eel, heal, heel, he'll, keel, kneel, meal, peel, peal, reel, real, seal, steal, spiel, squeal, she'll, wheel....*

"How many of you can think up a five-stress line to go underneath what we already have on the board that you can pull into place with one of the rhyme words on our sheet? It can be a continuation of the thought, 'I think I really don't know how I feel', or it can start a completely new sentence. In either case, it needs to move the image, thought, or feeling of the first line forward in some way. Let the rhyme word be the locomotive that pulls the rest of the line (like a freight train) along behind it and puts it on the right track.

"Remember, before you raise your hand, test each new trial line by writing it down, drumming the syllable and stress counts on your fingers with one hand, while whispering it into your other hand cupped to your ear. Listen to its rhythm! Write with your ears! Write with your whole body. Get into it — but try not to disturb others!"

Give students a few quiet minutes to probe their feelings, and try out the images or actions which will best express them....

"If I said 'Like it,'" a male voice may say, "all the jocks would squeal on me — they'd laugh and laugh and laugh at me."

Write this up on the board adjacent to the first line (but not yet under it). Ask for more trial responses, and put them up. Test each for metrical rhythm by speaking it aloud. Invite individuals in the class to weigh in on which fits best the rhythm and can move the first line forward. Then write the best new line under the first one already up.

```
ta-TUM  ta- TUM  ta-TUM  ta- TUM     ta-  TUM
I  think  I    real  ly don't  know how    I    feel.
If  I    said "Like  it," all    the   jocks  would squeal
on  me — they'd laugh and laugh and    laugh   at    me.
```

"That's great! You gave us *two* lines. The first rhymes with feel (squeal). Plus, it is enjambed with a second that sets up a new rhyme word, 'me'. Now, everyone, give me words that rhyme with *me*." Start another newsprint rhyme sheet for **me**: *b, be, bee, c, d, e, fee, flee, free, flea, glee, he, key, knee, pea, sea, spree, she, ski, tea, tree, three....*

"Who can come up with a line which rhymes — "

"I'd rather take the stinger of a bee," another student offers.

"That's a great line. Other lines?" Add this and other trial lines to one side of the poem on the board. Select the most workable. "Let's go with the first." Add this line now beneath the poem the class is building.

> I think I really don't know how I feel.
> If I said "Like it" all the jocks would squeal
> on me — they'd laugh and laugh and laugh at me.
> I'd rather take the stinger of a bee.

Ask, "What's a bee sting *most like*? This line starts a new couplet, so it does not rhyme with the line above it."

"Its venom is most like a flaming fire," another voice offers.

"That's a good line. Others...? No? Then we'll go with this."

(Note: if students really get into it, and most are participating and nodding a consensus when a good line is offered, it may only slow the process to insist upon more multiple trial lines just to gain verbal participation. You will be the best judge of this.)

> I think I really don't know how I feel.
> If I said "Like it" all the jocks would squeal
> on me — they'd laugh and laugh and laugh at me.
> I'd rather take the stinger of a bee.
> Its venom is most like a flaming fire

"Now, give me rhyme words that go with *fire.*" List them as they call them out: *Choir, dire, hire, ire, mire, spire, tire, wire....*

"Who has a five-stress line? Someone who hasn't participated yet...."

"So hot I'd slather it with cold wet mire," a voice calls out.

"Super! We're on a roll here! Other suggestions...? We're doing great work today! We'll add that as another line enjambed with the one above it." Add the line now.

"Is there more to the poem that it wants to say? Is there more we should add...? No? While you're thinking:

"Do you see the simile? *LIKE a flaming fire?* What if we made this a metaphor? Could we take out the words 'most' and 'like' to make room in our metrical line for a word that could imply the bee's stinger? Let's say, with the verb 'needle'? What could we write?"

"Its venom needles me with flaming fire?" a voice questions.

"Great! Everyone see what is happening here? See how your last contribution turned a simile into a metaphor? Questions? Who has an alternative metaphor? No one? Okay, let's go with this":

I think I really don't know how I feel.
If I said "Like it" all the jocks would squeal
on me — they'd laugh and laugh and laugh at me.
I'd rather take the stinger of a bee.
Its venom *needles* me with flaming fire
so hot I'd slather it with cold wet mire.

"Now we have a metaphor. Its venom is no longer *like* a flaming fire. It *is* a flaming fire that needles me. It **needles** *me with flaming fire.* The needling and the flaming fire are in effect *a single entity* in this metaphor. How did we do it? By removing the 'like' and compressing the line, we found space and a rhythmic fit allowing us to add the active verb 'needles' (for the stinger) which turned the simile into a metaphor.

"I see a hand raised in the back. Yes."

"The bee's fire, in three days, will go away. My closest buddy's ha-ha's here to stay."

"Excellent. And, sadly, true! Let's add those lines to the poem, and also give it a title."

Add the last two lines under the poem.

"We wouldn't serve the poem well if we called it 'How Do I

24

Feel About Poetry?' because that gives the poem away too quickly. It is better to employ some expression of its most central metaphor in the title. When we do, we find it adds dimension to the poem. We call the use of the central metaphor in the title a 'Constituting Metaphor'.

"Also, a sub-text line or two between the title and the first line of the poem will often help ease the reader into the situation of the poem by supplying a context, but still without giving the poem itself away. The full impact of the poem only becomes apparent in the final line, which gives it a strong close."

## NEEDLINGS

Q: How do you feel about poetry?
A:

I think I really don't know how I feel.
If I said "Like it" all the jocks would squeal
on me — they'd laugh and laugh and laugh at me.
I'd rather take the stinger of a bee.
Its venom needles me with flaming fire
so hot I'd slather it with cold, wet mire.
The bee's fire, in three days, will go away.
My closest buddy's *ha-ha*'s here to stay.

"Thus rhymes have led us to lines, lines to a simile, the simile to a metaphor central to the poem, and that to a 'constituting metaphor' title."

****

Notice, in all this, that we do *not* start with a preconception of the subject matter of the poem to be crafted. We do *not* make a poem-crafting assignment by saying, "Write on a topic of interest to you." (Panic: "But I can't think of anything." How many times have you heard that? Or yourself felt that way?) *Nor* do we say, "Write about topic 'X.'" That only limits the imagination to "X" and fixates it there.

We start, instead, with a single *feeling line* ending in a word that has **rhymes enough** *to give the poem freedom to move in a direction towards the coherence that it "seems to want."* The poem-makers, whether as students in a class or a small group — sensitive to

25

the feeling that is emerging in each line — *follow* the emerging poem, line by line, to its coherent conclusion in a final line.

It works the same way for an *individual* who is crafting a poem *alone.* The individual poem-maker, *sensitive to the feeling that is emerging in the poem, follows it to its coherent conclusion* — often to a surprising new sunny place of discovery.

It all starts with authentic feeling and is developed through the underlying metrical beat, plus the music of end rhymes, as you write out loud on your fingers to your ears. Metrical rhyming poetry helps us get in touch with our feelings in a way that is almost magical because it accesses the more creative, more subtle, right hemisphere.

You can gauge your students' comprehension by how fully they participate. You may wish to use several class sessions, the latter of them for doing individual solo work utilizing rhyme sheets already accumulated in group work. When finished, invite students to share their best poems by reading them before the class.

The solo work will help prepare them to craft a poem for homework, where they will be working individually by themselves without needing your help or that of their classmates or parents.

(Poets-to-be: I trust that while my attention has been on the teacher in this chapter, it has become clear to you how you are to participate by following closely and executing, step by step as directed, the instructions the teacher gives to students in the imaginary class. Be sure you have also utilized all the "7 Write-downs" of your own listed at the beginning of this chapter. Put all the results in your three-ring binder.)

# 4. Sensing Resistance to Poetry?

You will sometimes sense resistance to poetry on the part of a number of students, especially "macho" males, who may express their feelings non-verbally, or by saying things like,

"To me, writing these verses just plain sucks."

Convert this kind of negative energy into positive momentum. Rather than resist the thrust, pull it, and the student with it, towards you by saying something to him like:

"That could be a pretty good first line: 'To me, writing these verses just plain sucks.'" Put this up on the board verbatim, and above it write your "ta-TUMs" (as illustrated in the preceding chapter, but in this case irregular) where everyone can see them and get involved.

ta-TUM *TUM- ta*    ta- TUM  ta- TUM  ta- TUM
To me,  writ  ing these ver  ses just  plain sucks.

Point out the stresses. (Let me elaborate: This line is an *irregular* iambic pentameter line. It is important to accept it because it is what the resistant student offered, and it is perfectly good diction, even if it is "street talk" and not "poetic." (The important thing is that it expresses real feeling. *It's real feeling you want to run with.*)

Irregular "feet" (reverse ta-TUMs) need to come early in the line so the reader or hearer has a chance to recover the regular rhythm by the end of it. This line will work well in that respect. However, you need for the next line to be regular, in order securely to re-establish and sustain the basic meter:

ta-TUM *TUM- ta*    ta- TUM  ta- TUM  ta- TUM
To me,  writ  ing these ver  ses just  plain sucks.
ta-TUM   ta-TUM   ta-TUM   ta-TUM   ta-TUM

(However, if there is *no* metrical coherence to the line, you need to ask for the student's agreement to make the fewest possible rhythmic changes that will let it match one of the metrical lines above.)

"Now, everyone, give me all the words you can think up that rhyme with sucks." Put them up on a rhyme sheet taped to the board where everyone can see it. ***Sucks:*** *bucks, chucks, clucks, ducks, mucks, plucks, pucks, shucks, trucks, tucks....*

"So, to you, writing these verses just plain sucks. What kind of sucking sound does it make? Listen closely — everyone — in your imagination: *What's the sound most LIKE?* See if someone can give me a *regular* five-stress line with a simile, introduced by the word 'like', that ends with one of those rhyme words."

Remind your students to try out each provisional line by drumming the desk top with the fingers of one hand while cupping the other hand to one ear and whispering into it. Thus they are writing it out loud with lips, fingers and ears. Give them time to feel, and to think, and to come up with multiple trials while you hand out written instructions in outline form as recommended in the preceding chapter.

"Like rear-compacting crunch-up garbage trucks," someone offers from the back of the room.

"Like slurping septic system pumper trucks," another student, a pal of the resistant one, offers. (Laughter).

"I'd rather Dad and I went shooting ducks," the resistant student offers with a surprising change in tone.

Write *all* their trial responses to one side, on the board. Note that the idea is to go with what the students offer, and what is also most useful to the poem. The idea is *not,* at this point, to go with what is most decorous and tasteful in the mind of an adult.

"We could go with either the first or the second one here because each offers a good simile. However, the second simile works better — 'suck' to 'slurp' is a smoother sensory image transition than 'suck' to 'crunch', which is different in kind. The slurping image is interesting because it's not the first thing that might come to mind. You've exercised good imagination. It's a good five-stress line.

"Or, we could go with the third, which is also a good five-stress line. It would change the direction in which the poem is moving, and that's okay to do this early in the poem. Which would *you* prefer?" Direct this question to the resistant student. He is the one you most want to draw out, and a change in his tone is now apparent.

"Let's go with the ducks," he says with a half-smile.

(That the resistant student has ignored your request for a simile in the line is less important than that he is emerging from his resistant shell. Accept what he offers. You have more lines coming to find the similes you need to demonstrate how metaphors work.)

"So, now we've got a couplet, two lines that rhyme":

```
ta- TUM TUM- ta   ta-   TUM ta- TUM ta-   TUM
To me,  writ ing these ver  ses just  plain sucks.
ta- TUM ta-  TUM ta- TUM ta-  TUM ta- TUM
I'd rath  er   Dad  and I    went shoot ing ducks.
```

"Who can add another line with a simile to the poem? This line does not have to rhyme, since we are starting a new couplet."

"I'd rather fall into the marshy drink" another student offers. Write this trial line up on the board, to the side.

"That's a good image! Now, those who haven't participated, give me more five-stress lines that use a simile, that is, an image that is like another image, introduced by 'like.'"

"I'd rather rot, like dead birds in the drink" a voice offers.

"That's pretty good. It's a good simile, too. Any other offerings...? No? Sure?"

"That's a good line. Let's use that line!" the resistant student says, his voice rising with interest.

```
ta- TUM TUM- ta   ta-   TUM ta- TUM ta-   TUM
To me,  writ ing these ver  ses just  plain sucks.
ta- TUM ta-  TUM ta- TUM ta-  TUM ta- TUM
I'd rath  er   Dad  and I    went shoot ing ducks.
I'd rath  er   rot  like dead birds in  the    drink
```

"Now, give me all the words you can that rhyme with *drink*." List on a fresh sheet what the class offers: **drink:** *clink, blink, brink, ink, kink, link, pink, stink, think, wink....*

"So, we've got a couplet and a third line. Who can think of a five-stress line with a simile which ends with a rhyme on *drink*?"

"Than quack rhymed lines, like bird rot, that just stink," another offers.

"Good for you! You just gave us an instinctively appropriate metaphor in the verb 'quack'! Any more suggestions...? No? Sure?" Put this under the three lines already there. Congratulate them all on using imagination to come up with a rhyming 'simile poem'.

"Here's the poem with similes in lines three and four."

To me, writing these verses just plain sucks.
I'd rather Dad and I went shooting ducks.
I'd rather rot, *like dead birds* in the drink

than quack rhymed lines, *like bird rot*, that just stink.

"Let's find more metaphors.  What if the rotting in line 3 wasn't just *like* the rot of birds in the drink, but **was** *a rotting bird, or its action, or the result of that action?* How can we convert this simile into a metaphor? Suggestions...? No? Watch closely.  In line three we drop the 'like' and substitute for the simile *'like dead birds'*, the metaphor, in *apposition* to the speaker:

"I'd rather *rot — a dead duck —* in the drink.

"Note, we make *birds* singular, to agree with the speaker (singular), and make the species a duck, specific, to fit the context.

"The speaker is no longer saying he'd rather rot *like dead birds* but that he would rather **be** *a dead duck rotting.*

"And we can, in line four, anchor our sense of place, and compress *quack rhymed lines, like bird rot,* from a likeness to an identity, thus —

*"than rot in class, and quack-quack rhymes that stink!*

"The poem's  speaker is not writing rhymed lines which are *like* bird rot.  Instead, he is saying now that he is so much identified with a dead  duck that he is speaking as only (live) ducks can speak. *He* is *rotting in class and quack-quacking rhymes that stink!* These steps compress the lines' imagery and make them more powerful by substituting, for a mere likeness, a vigorous movement with action verbs that create, in each case, *an identity*.

"Moreover, we have done it by enjambing lines three and four, which make a single sentence.  The two lines are read without a pause. That adds interest to the poem and speeds it to a dramatic close after the first two lines, which are end-stopped with periods.

"Questions at this point...?  Here's our 'metaphor poem'":

To me, writing these verses just plain sucks.
I'd rather Dad and I went shooting ducks.
I'd rather rot, a dead duck, in the drink
than rot in class, and quack-quack rhymes that stink!

"Rhymes lead to lines, lines to similes, similes to metaphors.

"Can we come up with a title for the poem?  A constituting metaphor title?  Remember, a constituting metaphor is one so central to the poem that it can stand in the reader's eye and memory for the whole poem...." The class is silent. " No takers at all?"  (They know the bell is about to ring, ending the period. So do you.) "How's this?"

## DEAD DUCK QUACK

To me, writing these verses just plain sucks.
I'd rather Dad and I went shooting ducks.
I'd rather rot, a dead duck, in the drink
than rot in class, and quack-quack rhymes that stink.

****

I trust this gives you an idea about how you may be open to *expressions of resistance*, and to recognize them when they are voiced (or perhaps suppressed until you draw them out). Handle resistance in a structured way that accepts a student who is struggling internally with it. (It may be quite dark.) This approach will engage him and other students as well, and advance the learning objectives of the exercise for the whole class when you manage it well.

If you get into this kind of encounter, which is superficially "negative," you need also to reward your more positive-minded students. If you encourage it in advance, many of them will have written one or more couplets of their own while you have been working so closely with the resistant student. You will get a variety of feelings on the same or similar subjects expressed in their couplets. Review these, and invite the authors of the best to put them up on the board. Thus you can close the session with balance, representing, more broadly, most of the students in the class.

**Here's What You've Accomplished:**
1) In the second class, you've met a resistant student where he is, and accepted what he has to offer on a feeling level. It is by no means everybody's poem. It is an unusually dark poem. It lacks layered meanings and its depth is discovered in a single reading. However, you've engaged him at a deeply significant level of acceptance, in the darkness of his feeling. Your acceptance, and that of the class — all sharing his darkness to some extent — just might someday make a poet of him.
2) In both classes, you've got most students participating, competing in a relaxed, friendly, and cooperative way with each other.
3) You have led both classes through the first principle of

31

Reverse Rhyming. This is to help the poet-to-be to get past the crisis of "what to write a poem about" by starting with *any* metrical line that carries *authentic* warmth and feeling.

4) You've helped students discover, for the second and following lines of a poem, *how to find a rhyme first, and let it pull the new line into place beneath it.* Thus they have by-passed the crisis of finding unforced rhymes which "work." They've discovered how they can make couplets with true ear rhymes of naturally flowing speech.

5) You've helped them furnish the poems with similes by asking "like what?" to develop rich colorful images.

6) You have demonstrated how students may turn their similes into metaphors by dropping the "like" and substituting an active verb or verb phrase to turn the likeness into an identity, and to tighten the metrical line with specific action as they do.

7) You have shown students the application of central metaphors to constituting metaphor titles.

8) What your students have learned to do in the classroom each can do individually, working alone, or in small groups. Thus, you have imparted to them the rudiments of a pleasurable life-skill each can pursue as a pass-time, for a lifetime — perhaps even as a "calling." Your students' satisfaction will grow richer and more gratifying with practice as each grows and acquires more sophistication in it.

## In Conclusion

It really is remarkably easy to make a "metaphor poem" by reverse rhyming once you surrender yourself to its rhythms long enough to get the hang of it and give up the effort to over-control the outcome as to "what the poem is about." Thus started, the poem will virtually compose itself. You have only to follow with sensitivity where it wants to go for maximum coherence.

Rhyming your way to 'metaphor poems' integrates the right and left hemispheres of the brain with surprisingly musical and rhythmic pleasures for the ear. This pleases poet, reader and audience. That's why "formal" verse has lasted so many centuries in so many different languages despite the intricacies of its composition. (For more of the "Whys" see Chapter 7.)

I personally know of no joy quite comparable to it. It's my hope that you also can experience it for yourselves, and impart a similar appreciation to your students.

# 5. Fourteen Poems for Fun and Instruction

from
*21ST CENTURY BREAD: SHORT RHYMING POEMS POST-9/11*
Copyright © 2007 by Leland Jamieson

## Against All Odds

Early September.
Oklahoma City to Memphis via The Rock Island Rocket.
Memphis to Asheville via Southern Railroad.


The upper berth lurched hard from side to side.
Her wheels of steel — click-clack, click-clack astride
her groaning rails and ties, their changing pitch,
that syncopation past a side-rail switch —
would normally have zonked him out at once,
except he feared that he'd be made class dunce.

Suppose they would not hold the seven-ten
departure, Memphis-bound-for-Asheville, when
the Rock Island Rocket ran a little late?
They said they would, but what if they'd not wait?
He'd miss the Old Boys' Deadline — be a chump!
The thought turned his whole throat into a lump . . . .

First off the platform, he inquired, "The train
for Asheville?" "Sonny, there she rolls.  Retain
your ticket.  It is good tomorrow too."
He lurched his suitcase up, and sprinting, drew
abreast the last car's Lookout post and rail,
scrambled down concrete steps — he dared not fail!

Again he breasted the Lookout post, rail, stair,
grabbed the post, vaulted bag and butt through air,
and landed, teetering.  He crawled up-tread,
stood rocking, guts and knees like gingerbread.
The door: locked tight!  What could he do?  Good Lord!
Up high, 'Emergency!'  He pulled the cord.

Shrieking, the train stopped dead.  Look, men with bags
raced by, their footfalls crunching clinker slags.
He jumped down, ran, caught up, and with them climbed
up through the diner's elevator (slimed
with swill from stinking barrels he pushed by),
and passed a black-faced cook with a knowing eye.

Pretending calm he bumped his bag up-aisle.
"Not taken," said a kid his age (thin smile).
"Oh.  Thanks."  He gasped for breath, his thudding heart
impatient now to see the train depart
lest someone find him out — throw him in jail —
and who in Memphis would, for him, pay bail?

"You're really out of breath!" this Thin Smile said.
He nodded, "Out of shape."  His face burned red.
He wedged his ticket in the front seat's back,
reclined, eyes closed, and lay upon the rack
of his anxiety until he felt
a forward lurch.  His fear began to melt . . . .

Steel wheels and rails were singing when he woke.
A stub, no ticket, wedged the seat back's yoke.
(Thin Smile gazed out, his head against the glass.)
The mountains heaved in view, in greening mass,
and singing wheels on rails dropped down in pitch.
He stretched his forearm, kneading out a twitch.

Thin Smile turned great brown eyes toward him and grinned.
"While you were sleeping, this man — double-chinned —
stopped by to thank you, left his card for you.
Some lawyer, lives in Asheville, well-to-do."
"Thanked me?  For what?"  "He said that you would know.
Said twice, 'Magnifico!  Magnifico!'"

Thin Smile was chuckling, grinning ear to ear.
"I watched you panting, glimpsed a touch of fear,
observed you didn't want to talk at all.
No cobbler, I'd not twist a sharpened awl
to tap your guts, for curiosity —

you had to catch your breath.  I let you be.

"The lawyer, while you slept, described the scene —
said several men agreed they'd never seen
determination like your own to catch
this train — bold action which alone could snatch
a lost day back they thought was down the drain.
They all send 'Thanks!' for helping them entrain . . . .

"What was it drove you on, against all odds?"
"Still greater odds!  Drove me like piston rods!
I'm going back to boarding school, you see.
If I were late, I'd dig a stump, a tree
in fact, before I could return to sports —
I'd be class dunce, and off the tennis courts."

"You don't say!  That's not Christ School?  Could it be?"
"None other.  What?  You got telepathy?"
"I'm going there — read all about that stump
a really big dumb screw-up makes you hump."
"Well! — let me welcome you.  Name's Jamieson."
They shook hands, soberly.  "Mine's Bateyson."


## Silage Team — Machete Thirst

Early September.  Working Christ School's farm, in a rich
mountain bottom south of Asheville, North Carolina.

My eyes sweat thorns.  They're filled with grit, air-borne
on every swipe of blade.  I think they'll burst.
Nothing is worse than cutting ripened corn —
no work I ever did brought me such thirst —
or are the bug bites down my shirt the worst . . . ?
Come truck ride in, atop the load, we skin
and munch green stalks — how broad and sweet each grin!

# Rapture in the Sun

In memory of E.T.P.
DeLand, Florida.


The navel oranges Mom arranged
in her fresh centerpiece I changed
but slightly, picking one to eat
because it looked to be so sweet.

I salivated as I probed
my thumbnail in the rind that robed
the paler plugs inside of it,
spraying the sunlit air, flit by flit.

The rind-oil misted both my hands
with passion only Sun commands.
Inhaled, it was intoxicating . . . .
The quenching plugs?  Ah . . . .   Captivating!


# Jalopy's Gift

In memory of E.T.P.


Come summer evenings in DeLand, we three
(my step-dad, fifty, Momma soon to be,
and I, fifteen), iced drinks in hands, would rock
in wicker chairs on our front porch and talk.
A Harley filled my mind and heart and maw,
but Papa said most drivers never saw
a bike until they hit and killed the rider —
impaled, or thrown, or squashed like some poor spider.

So he proposed he buy a sweet jalopy —
if I would fix it up and not be sloppy,
and help to pay for what would make it hum
with summer work it'd take me to and from.

36

But I would have to understand it'd be,
though mostly mine, Mom's too, to use as she
sometimes required, a second car she'd drive
on errands, on a schedule we'd contrive.

"A deal!" I cried. We bought a Model A,
a '31, a Coup Cabriolet,
the wooden roof frame rotted, fabric gone,
no floor, its seats the jaws of a mastodon.
I made mechanical repairs, cut out
of plywood brand new floorboards nice and stout,
engaged a cabinet-maker to frame the roof,
and shellacked it well to make it moisture-proof.

Then Mom, who knew the re-upholstery game,
stretched sewing tape across our new roof frame,
and laid out canvas free of any seam
except for one we'd tack down on each beam.
She must have stuck a thousand pins in it,
until, as smooth as a baseball cap, it fit.
On her machine she stitched each seam with class.
She marked, and I installed, the rear view glass.

We stretched it on. While she snugged tight the slack
to smooth out wrinkles, I drove home each tack.
I sponged on water from the tap while hot,
and lickety-split — it dried up nice and taut.
With paintbrush I applied a mold-proof white —
deck paint for boats — to make it watertight.
I masked the lines of tacks with braid for trim.
More paint filled braid and canvas to the brim.

Next, cushion springs. I learned Mom's tying knack.
A tough red vinyl covered seat and back,
each trimmed with vivid yellow piping, bright
and cheerful — the doors the same — to my delight.
Now weather-tight, interior done, I sanded
the rusted body spots — until I landed
on shiny steel I primed to hold rust back.
I cross-brushed on two coats of gleaming black . . . .

Mom threw herself into the sewing whir.
I had not guessed she had it still in her,
especially when I think of her gnarled fingers . . . .
What was the greatest joy? — the gift that lingers . . . ?
Perhaps the strife it helped us jettison:
of age, of sex, of roles of mother and son
each grieving loss in a private paradigm . . . .
We lived and worked together in present time.


## Boiler Man

Winter, Christ School, Fifth Cottage, in the mountains
south of Asheville, North Carolina.


He shut his eyes — a happy lad.
Slow warmth suffused his back porch bed.
Boiler men's lives were not so bad!
He'd won, fifth form, the thoroughbred
of boilers 'cause he'd kept his head
on lesser jobs — pulled clinkers small,
flushed water feeds, punched tubes and all . . . .

He woke . . . . Could not evoke the dream
that stirred him with such urgency.
Was two A.M., said watch hands' gleam.
He stretched — was snug as could be,
but couldn't shake himself quite free
this pressing sense that he must rise.
Some dopey dream! He closed his eyes.

How cold was it? He clawed his nails
against the poncho's underside
and scraped off ice like soft fish scales.
He tossed. Such restlessness! He sighed.
He grabbed his flashlight for a guide,
slid loafers on, strode through the door
and stepped upon a creaking floor.

38

The strongest scent of turpentine
pervaded bath and cottage hall!
So hot!  A chill went up his spine.
He squatted, palmed the floor and wall.
Hot floor?  His dream!  A psychic call?
He strode outside and hung a left.
The cellar door was stuck.  More heft!

He kicked it open.  A dim red glow!
White vapor — turpentine — flowed out
across his flashlight's feeble throw:
He fought against an instant doubt —
a light-switch spark?  Another route?
What if the time it took to wake
eight sleepers up's too much to take?

He flipped the switch.  Two bulbs went on.
In their dim light he just could see
the whole surreal phenomenon
(his last year's job) — the big Square D
cut-off, on the coal bin's post, should be
there still, behind that old Mae West.
With fresh night air he filled his chest.

Halfway across the packed-clay floor
he tripped, and sprawled, and spilled his air.
He gasped for breath, spit clay, and swore.
Back on his feet, he gripped the Square
D cut-off — yanked it with a prayer . . . .
Thank God we didn't blow sky high!
He dropped to the clay's fresh air supply.

On hands and knees, with worm's eye view
he thanked the stoker's dying whine.
He gazed — while the fire box door changed hue
from bright orange-red's near-molten shine
to graying blue's most welcome sign . . . .
Three giant pine knots in a beam
dripped pitch on it — sizzling to steam.

# Springing Formal Tongues

"The poet who imposes rhyme at ends of lines just complicates his task," said Freeverse. "Burns up time!  Forget those wind-chimes rhyme creates.  Dismiss that breeze which captivates, you say, one's ears and nose and eyes.  Throw out those rhymes in senses' guise.

"What is mere
pleasure
in your stress of speech
*against*
your 'feet,'
your 'line'?
I hear a sing-song voice —
or less.
I sleep.
Ta-TUM-ta's anodyne!
Don't ask me drone
ta-TUM-ta's whine.
Far better that I vote with feet.
Give me potatoes.
Give me meat."

I said to Freeverse, "Think!  Make sense!
It's speech-stress springs the formal tongue
and heaves into the breeze its scents
and sights, its ear's delights — when wrung
from pulsing lines the poet's strung.
You hold in hand the poem, whole.
You feel its heartbeat, sense its soul.

"So you must dare to read with flair!
No formal poem's a travel guide
in broken prose — look *here,* look *there!*
We need your conscious full-length stride
to call up feeling pain would hide,
strike water from the rock of doubt —
and heal our wounds from inside out!"

# Scrabbling for Scarlet Oaks

A poet scrabbles in his Mother Tongue,
lays down not words with letters scoring high,
but lines of words to hear what's not yet sung
which — ringing true — will need no alibi.
With serendipity he stumbles on
those sensate words that rhyming lines evoke,
with images a meter spawns: clear-drawn
rough acorns which prefigure scarlet oak.

A reader reads across the meter's beat
with speech-stress sounding cadenced counterpoint
inviting heart and mind to dance with feet.
The scrabbler's and the reader's work — conjoint —
conspire, creating out of clear bold air,
with Mother Tongue, her foursquare oak, *mon cher*.


# Formal Poet as a Rooster

As a violin beneath one's jaw
will resonate in the conch of ear,
spread gooseflesh through the player's maw,
electrify his chakras' sphere,
impel him toward a right-brained awe —
so may a formal chanticleer.

The horsehair bow of reading stress
contests each line — articulates
what's drawn across pentam or less
(tetram or trim) — and celebrates
new vibes that "free verse" can't express.
What un-taut string reverberates?

It's speech-stress firing at the breech
ignites taut measured lines' end chimes,
push-pulls at sense with feeling's reach —

as poet (reader, hearer) times
out moss-thick tongues, cliché-gray speech,
and cries up dew-fresh paradigms.


## Void of White

The void of white — before that first
impression hands have not rehearsed,

before the voice has found its chords
or fingers beat their keys to swords,

before each moves, creates anew —
most deeply frightens me.  And you?


## Arcs of Quarks?

What is this pleasure, making poems
from tabula rasa, from scratch?
From void's deep nothingness, what homes
upon the sentient being's thatch?
What lights it like a flaming match
and would consume it — yet ignites,
with grace, these words by bits and bytes?

What paces heart, darts inner eye,
reverbs in mind, rebounds from brain
through pen or keyboard fingers ply?
What vibes try voice cords, give free rein
to bone-and-air-wave ears' domain?
What Zero Point Field's "found-gone" quarks
delight us with their blinking arcs?

# From a Long Pig's Pen

A fellow asked me once, "What makes you tick?
Expressed in *three* words, neither more nor less?"
You'd think I'd know all my own bailiwick
but I'd not thought it through, I must confess.
No thoughts or feelings would stay put — I roped
and hog-tied lots of them, but most dodged off
my cagey pen, while others interloped.
So I gave up the game of philosophe.

The rods and cones of it come down to this:
By letting go obsessive hot pursuit
I draw myself away from that abyss
to slanting light, capricious breezes, a route:
Blank paper, meter, rhyme — so frangible —
my three are *seeing, making tangible.*


# Form as Kindling

A poet may seek less from speech than embers,
from smoldering coals that shrink on his gray grate
until, with kindling, he some flame remembers.
What heartbeat-metered lines accelerate
his unsung Mother Tongue will celebrate
when inner chimes draw her to life with rhyme
well-matching both his past, and present, time.


# Dance of the Quivering Digits

For Savannah and her friends. April, 2005.

When thought and feeling don't pan out,
does your heart throb with aching doubt?
You fear that you will never write

43

another line that feels quite right?
Then drum your fingers, and find "feet"
to dance the line your digits beat!

Next, find a rhyme word that can pull
a second line (one trim but full)
from heart and mind and quivering hand
*whether or not it's what you "planned."*
When once you've got two lines that dance,
across your lips quick smiles will prance.

Where do these two lines want to go?
How step aside and let them flow?
If you rely on feet and rhyme
they'll find you more lines, every time.
Say "Yes!" to their uncanny smarts —
well known for warming poets' hearts!

They'll often lead you to express
a thought or feeling with finesse
you did not know you had in you
until the rhyme pulled it in view.
Thus, you may open inner eyes
to see what's true — for you.  Surprise!


## Formal Poet as a Whittler

The poet grips a block of oak
and chips at it with chiming blade
by feel, for rhymes it may evoke.
The lyric heft in hand is weighed
for spirit's shapely escapade,
for fragrant lines that guide the eye
and ear — and voice to sing thereby.

# 6. Similes and Metaphors Defined and Identified

Now that we've demonstrated in chapters 3 and 4 a few of the intricacies of the interplay of similes and metaphors in relation to the metrical line, let's define them formally and take a close look at those found in the 14 poems in the preceding chapter. This will give you a broader frame of reference.

We'll look first at Merriam-Webster's Collegiate Dictionary, 11th Edition, to define and compare the two terms:

**A Simile** is "a figure of speech comparing two unlike things that is often introduced by *like* or *as* ([e.g.]... *cheeks like roses*)."

**A Metaphor** is "a figure of speech in which a word or phrase literally denoting one kind of object or idea is used in place of another to suggest a likeness or analogy between them ([e.g.]... *drowning in money*)...."

What's the practical difference? Whereas the simile is "her cheeks are LIKE roses," the metaphor is *"her cheeks ARE roses."*

Whereas similes are most often introduced by "like" or "as," in the case of metaphors there is no introductory "like" or "as." *The metaphor is used in place of the simile.* Moreover, the poem-maker is not merely drawing a comparison between two unlike things that have, nevertheless, some kind of likeness. He or she is pressing the argument further than that, and saying that *the one is, or has become, or is acting as the other. It IS the other* in some important aspect. Again, Her cheeks ARE roses.

As shown in chapters 3 and 4 above, many similes become metaphors in the process of making a poem. Here, for example, the simile "Her cheeks are like roses" may become the metaphor "her cheeks are roses" as follows: The poet, in crafting the line for better rhythm, can decide to compress it and make it shorter and stronger. He just drops the word "like" and substitutes for it an active verbal phrase. What could be more simple in concept? (Of course, in practice, it can get a bit more complicated as one works out the line's metrical feet. We've taken a closer look at this several times in the chapters above.)

**A Constituting Metaphor** may be defined as a metaphor central to the understanding, feeling, or argument of the poem. When explicated by the work in its entirety, it embraces it wholly, or almost wholly. It can, as a single image in the reader's memory, stand for the *entire* poem. A Constituting Metaphor often functions as the title of the piece, as it does in "Dance of the Quivering Digits."

**Similes (S) and Metaphors (M) Identified for Each Poem:**

Poets-to-be, for greatest benefit, will want make a spirited effort to identify all the metaphors they can for themselves in the illustrative poems before looking at this checklist for confirmation.

Occurrences are listed by poem titles, in alphabetical order. Each instance of a simile or metaphor is separated by a comma. The metaphors far outweigh the similes. A metaphor, more compressed than a simile, lends itself well to the short condensed lines that characterize most rhyming poetry, especially lyric poems. These usually proceed at a leisurely pace, which gives the reader time to think about the layered implications of the metaphors. Most good metaphors are layered in meaning, many revealing these layers only on subsequent readings.

On the other hand, poems which tell a story with a strong narrative that rushes the reader along often have fewer metaphors than more reflective lyric poems, except in those stanzas where they take a pause in the action for reflection.

Here, for your thought and analysis, are similes and metaphors (both single words and phrases) that you may have identified in the Fourteen Poems. Perhaps there are some you have missed. You may disagree with some. You may find in the poems some I overlooked. Poets-to-be in a group or classroom should feel free to discuss and argue them. Two questions to bear in mind: 1) "What does each metaphor depict, a) literally, and b) figuratively?" 2) "Which of the titles, in your mind, best achieve the status of a Constituting Metaphor?" If you are working alone, write your answers down, review them, and when satisfied with this stage of your study, file them in your binder.

**Against All Odds: S:** Like piston rods; **M:** Syncopation past a side rail switch, breasted the Lookout post, vaulted bag and butt, bumped his bag, rack of his anxiety, fear began to melt, wheels and rails were singing, twist a sharpened awl, snatch a lost day back.

**Arcs of Quarks? S:** Like a flaming match; **M:** Tabula rasa, void's deep nothingness, thatch, bits and bytes, darts inner eye, ply, bone-and-air-wave ears' domain, "found-gone" quarks.

**Boiler Man: S:** Like soft fish scales; **M:** Thoroughbred of boilers, clawed his nails, spilled his air, with worm's eye view.

**Dance of the Quivering Digits: M:** Feet to dance the line, two lines that dance, prance, uncanny smarts, rhyme pulled it in view.

**Form as Kindling: M:** Embers, gray grate, flame remembers, heartbeat-metered lines, inner chimes.

**Formal Poet as a Whittler: M:** Block of oak, chips, chiming blade by feel, lyric heft in hand, weighted, spirit's shapely escapade.

**Formal Poet as a Rooster: S:** As a violin; **M:** Conch of ear, chakras' sphere, right-brained awe, horsehair bow of reading stress, contests each line, vibes that "free verse" can't express, speech-stress firing at the breech, ignites taut measured lines' end chimes, push-pulls at sense with feeling's reach, dew-fresh paradigms.

**From a Long Pig's Pen: M:** Long pig, pen, bailiwick, roped and hog-tied, cagey pen, rods and cones, abyss, slanting light.

**Jalopy's Gift: S:** Like some poor spider, as a baseball cap; **M:** Jaws of a mastodon, drove home, paint filled braid and canvas to the brim, landed on shiny steel, strife it helped us jettison.

**Rapture in the Sun: M:** Robed the paler plugs, passion only sun commands.

**Scrabbling for Scarlet Oaks: M:** Scrabbles in his Mother Tongue, lines... to hear what's not yet sung, need no alibi, images a meter spawns, meter's beat, cadenced counterpoint, heart and mind to dance, foursquare oak.

**Silage Team — Machete Thirst: M:** Machete thirst, eyes sweat thorns.

**Springing Formal Tongues: M:** Wind-chimes, against your feet, springs the formal tongue, heaves, scents and sights, ear's delights, wrung from pulsing lines the poet's strung, feel its heartbeat, travel guide, full-length stride, strike water from the rock of doubt.

**Void of White: M:** Impression hands have not rehearsed, voice has found its chords, fingers beat their keys to swords.

# 7. Why Line?  Why Meter?  Why Rhyme?

With nearly a century and a half of various forms of free verse in American poetry behind us, it is pertinent for the poet-to-be to ask, "Why, in the 21st Century, compose by line, or in meter, or in rhyme? Is this a reactionary throw-back to the 19th Century?"

Chapters 3-4 modeled many of the practical "whats" and "hows," of *composing* by the line, in meter, and in the ear-pleasing music of end-rhymes.

In this chapter, at the risk of over-simplification, I will summarize in my own words, to the extent it is pertinent to our subject, recent scientific thinking on the effects of line, meter, and rhyme in poetry with regard to their *impact on the human brain.*

This is drawn from a rather long technical paper to which we are all indebted, "The Neural Lyre: Poetic Meter, the Brain, and Time," by Frederick Turner and Ernst Pöppel.  It is found in a collection of essays, *New Expansive Poetry,* edited by R.S. Gwynn.

What does a study of 18 different languages, including Ancient Greek, Celtic, Chinese, English, French, German, Hungarian, Italian, Japanese, Latin, Slavic, Spanish, Uralic — plus those of Zambia and New Guinea and others less well-known in the west — show they *all have in common? All* utilize, in their most memorable poetry, lines that are *a similar length in elapsed time when spoken.*

On the one hand, the line length in all these languages does not exceed the elapsed time that the conscious mind consumes as it speaks, grasps, and understands the line's content *within* what is called the "present moment of hearing."  On the other hand, the line is not so short that it allows other thoughts to intrude into the unconsumed "present moment of hearing."  The biological or "neural length" of this interval is roughly *3 seconds.*

It is no accident that Iambic Pentameter, five stresses spoken over ten syllables, is so well established in English.  Iambic Tetrameter, four stresses over eight syllables, is also well established, as is four-stress English Ballad meter.  Why?  Pentameter takes on average 3.3 seconds to speak, Tetrameter 2.4.  These are congruent with lower frequency brain waves associated with the brain's heightened creativity in the 3-second "present moment of hearing."

When reading metrical end-rhymed poetry aloud we are drawn in by the underlying (subtle, *not* overemphasized) metrical auditory rhythm (ta-TUM, ta-TUM, ta-TUM) as well as by periodic end-rhymes. Scientists say ***the brain is driven by them.*** These *auditory rhythmic drivers* measure out each "present moment of hearing." They bring about a cooperative feedback loop across the corpus callosum between the (reasoning-and-word) strength of the left hemisphere and the (feeling-and-image) strength of the right.

When the right and left hemispheres are united in this feedback loop, we experience our world more holistically (whether as poets composing a poem, or readers of it, or listeners to it). This is especially true for experience we consider ambiguous, contradictory, or multiple in its meanings. Purely analytic left-brain thinking alone cannot accomplish this holistic integration for us.

Metrical end-rhymed poetry helps us make sense of the world with all its contradictions at a depth prose cannot. Free verse, even with its rhetorical rhythms, fails as deeply as prose. The reason? Both prose and free verse lack *regularly recurring* auditory drivers (subliminal ta-TUMs and end-rhymes) which create the low frequency brain waves. It's these brain-waves that achieve the feedback loop and effect the optimum *integration* of the two hemispheres, or *entrainment*.

To repeat, and add a third element: First is the underlying rhythm of meter, an auditory driver. Second is the recurring rhyme-sound images that mark turnings at the ends of three-second lines, also auditory drivers. Now add the Third: The lyric voice with its contrapuntal and interpretative speech-stress. These three join forces subliminally. Together they harness for the reader the power of the whole brain. They enable it to become *entrained,* and thus to experience poetry at its deepest levels.

Thus, line, meter, and rhyme are far from a throwback to a prior era (whether the 19th Century, or Shakespeare's time, or the time of the Ancient Greeks and Romans). Composing by line, in meter, and in true ear rhyme (*neither in slant rhymes, nor in blank verse*) makes the most time-proven and universal poetry for one simple reason. According to the scientific evidence available to us, it creates a three-fold structure enabling speech to entrain the human brain, and therefore access it most holistically.

**An Exercise:** Re-read "Springing Formal Tongues." 1) Note the last stanza's rhyme scheme. 2) Count the ta-TUMs in each line of it. 3) Convert the first two "paragraphs" to the same number of ta-TUMs per line by writing them out as fresh 7-line stanzas on a piece of paper. 4) What do you observe? 5) What difference does this make in how you read them? Surprised?

50

# 8. A Few More Nuts, Bolts, and Benefits

### Foot and Metrical Line

(Let me preface this chapter by saying that this is not the time for us to get distracted by delving into the extensive technical language of prosody. All this can be studied to good advantage later, in the resources listed in the final chapter.) However, a few words are in order now both to identify more fully and to review the basic terms for the processes we have been using.

For our limited purposes, I should briefly define "foot" and "metrical line" as follows: a "foot" is a "ta-TUM" taken as a unit. A metrical line is a series of such units. A five-stress, five-foot, ten-syllable metrical line is called Pentameter:

ta-TUM ta-TUM ta-TUM ta-TUM ta-TUM

and two frequent variations in individual lines are:

TUM-ta ta-TUM ta-TUM ta-TUM ta-TUM    (and)
ta-TUM TUM-ta ta-TUM ta-TUM ta-TUM

Subtract a "ta-TUM" at the end and you make it a four-stress, four foot, eight syllable line called Tetrameter. These three particular lines are called Iambic because the stress is on the second syllable of the foot (apart from variations in individual lines). There are other feet and other metrical lines, but all that is for a later study.

It's important when composing poetry to keep meter in mind. Check out each provisional line by speaking it out loud with one hand cupped to your ear, and drumming it out with the fingers of the other hand. Let lips and fingers both speak to your ear. You do this to make sure the words fit your metrical line, with or without an occasional intentional variation. (Re-read "Dance of the Quivering Digits.")

Remember meter is the underlying background drumbeat — the rhythm section, as it were — against which the cadence of speech-stress plays. Speech-stress plays a jazz-like counterpoint, just as a vocalist or solo instrument would for instrumental music. Speech stress, ta-TUMs, and recurring end-rhymes (the latter two being auditory rhythmic drivers), make up the total *rhythmic* music of the poem. The *lyric* music of the poem is furnished by end-rhymes, and also by alliteration, assonance, and consonance. The last three you will study on your own, as recommended above.

The majority of young poets-to-be elect music with a strong rhythmic beat in the forefront or background of most of the instrumental and vocal music they enjoy. It should require no effort for you to catch on to the ta-TUMs, combined with the turns marked by end-rhymes, as the background rhythm in this special word-music which is metrical end-rhymed poetry.

This booklet is not a handbook on Prosody, and I think, with these homely non-technical illustrations, I've said enough for our purposes about foot and metrical line. For further reference, you may study with profit Timothy Steele's *All the Fun's in How You Say a Thing.* (See Chapter 10 for that and other reference titles.)

### Couplet

"Dance..." is an illustration of a poem crafted in couplets. A couplet is a pair of consecutive lines that share a rhyme. The rhyme scheme is AA, BB, CC and so on. It can be as short as two lines, or it can have as many paired lines as you want. The "narrative couplet" is one among several forms used in a longer poem that tells a story. Examples of these are "Against All Odds" and "Jalopy's Gift."

### Enjambment

Enjambment, or enjambed lines, occur when the thought is not contained completely in a single line but flows over into the next line *without a comma.* It is read *without a pause* between the lines. Shakespeare used it continuously in his dramatic verse. It is an important support that helps bring out speech-stress rhythms, which often run like a counterpoint to the metrical line, as stated above. Use it to keep your lines from being read in a sing-song voice and rhythm.

To support the reading of enjambed lines, it is necessary to *avoid capitalizations except for proper nouns and for the beginning of sentences,* rather than using them to start every line. When used to begin every line, capitalizations tend to interrupt and confuse an enjambed reading, when that occurs, by miscuing the eye.

### The Poem is Not an Essay, Theme, or Letter

Making a poem is not like writing an essay, theme, or letter. With them, you start with an idea, feeling, or conception (or even a full outline) of what you want to say, and the struggle is to find words that most faithfully express it.

In making a poem, you move in another direction. You start with any words best expressing warm, authentic feeling. Compose your first metrical line with these. Then you find multiple rhymes in your dictionary that randomly invite you down multiple paths. From these potentials you choose *one rhyme word with the line it generates* that is warmest and most exciting to follow, without too strong a notion of what the line should "say." *Your struggle is to recognize and keep faith with the coherence the poem wants to become.* It is not to keep faith with an outline or the words of your starting idea.

Let me repeat that for emphasis: *Your struggle is to recognize and keep faith with the coherence the poem wants to become.*

### Benefit: Reverse Rhyming Reduces Use of Clichés

At first you might be inclined to resist the idea of reverse rhyming, because to stop and look for rhyming words slows, if only a little, the rushing flow of your creative juices. However, your rush of creativity will not go away. Quite possibly that rush may be your biggest obstacle, since it is filling the void of creativity — *often with left-brain clichés* — before you have a chance to look and see what fresh, new, undiscovered imagery can randomly be drawn out of the void of the right hemisphere with a rhyme word that had not occurred to you from memory.

### Benefit: English *Is a* Rhyme-Rich Language

As I worked more and more with rhyme, I discovered English was not, after all, a rhyme-poor language — as my friends studying Italian mistakenly told me it was. English *is*, in fact, a rhyme-rich language. It's all the more fun because a relatively large number of words that rhyme with each other don't look at all alike. Examples are: *bite, byte, bright, Fahrenheit.* That's due to the Greek, Latin, Gaelic, Celtic, Germanic and Anglo-Saxon roots of English — due to words which are spelled so differently, and look so different. They surprise and delight the reader when they sound alike. The trick is to use those surprising delights to pull the poem forward. After the opening line, *first find the rhyme, then the next line.*

### Benefit: Sustaining Your Creativity

You'll probably never run completely dry as a poet if you follow a "sensory" variation on Natalie Goldberg's advice. In several of her many books devoted to creativity for writers, and to helping to overcome writer's block, she suggests making a list at random of ten nouns and fifteen verbs as follows: Number 1-15 down the *middle* of a sheet of paper. To the right of this column of numbers, list 15 random active verbs. To the left, list only ten random nouns. (No adjectives or adverbs are allowed.)

Use the verb on the right to make a sentence *in which the corresponding noun on the left serves either as the subject or object* of the verb. Verbs 1-10 work with nouns 1-10, and verbs 11-15 with nouns 1-5, so that those nouns get used twice. You have more verbs than nouns because verbs yield more pay dirt when you use the first 5 nouns a second time with different verbs.

As my own personal "sensory" variation on the Goldberg list, I impose on each sentence I write the additional requirement that it must speak to or through, or otherwise exhibit or utilize, one of the five senses. I require "sight" in lines 1, 6, 11; "hearing" or sound" in lines 2, 7, 12; "smell" in 3, 8, 13; "touch" in 4, 9, 14; and "taste" in 5,10, and 15. Thus I develop a set of sentences with rich sensory contact with the world as we experience it. This process almost never fails me. It often saves me from becoming blocked, or from becoming too intellectual and wrecking the poem!

I utilize this approach when I'm feeling dry and have no idea what to write about. I "mine" an ordinary dictionary page by page for familiar words commonly used, so they're random accept for alliteration.

On the other hand, if I have a desire to write on an event, or on a topic, sensation, intuitive feeling, or relationship, I free-associate all the nouns and active verbs I can think of that feel to me in some way connected with the subject of my interest. I make a "sensory" Goldberg list of these, and write the sentences. From the warmest I compose the first line of the poem. I hold "what the poem is about" at arm's length and let it come coherently into focus on its own as the *end-result,* not the cause of the writing. Often the resulting poem shows me something I was not even aware of when I began to compose, and is superior to any fleeting glimpses of it when I first started to muse on it.

Inventing and writing these often-difficult prose sentences can be hard work, due to the sense-criteria. Stick with it to the end to dig up from deep in your semi-consciousness those relationships which the exercise generates that are warm. Only these are suitable for re-composing into poetry that has depth for you. Sometimes one such

54

exercise will generate two or even three poems.

Poets-to-be have to be as honest as possible with themselves, and use only those results from this exercise which produce warmth of feeling. It is useless to try to approach a topic, "feeling," or subject that neither radiates warmth nor arouses passion in you. In view of this, I avoid scientific words because they leave me, personally, cold. I most like words with Celtic, Gaelic, French, German and Anglo-Saxon roots, words of one, two, or three syllables, because they are often warmer to me than words of many syllables with Latin roots. Words my stepfather used often are on this list, as are words frequently used by other members of my family and close friends.

Although I have well-developed intellectual and philosophical interests, and these sometimes intrude themselves into my work despite my "sensory" Goldberg list (and sometimes even get published), they don't make my best poetry, and probably won't yours.

Another matter to keep in your vigilant awareness: Our everyday language carries so much marketing jargon, and it is so loud and insistent in our ears, that it has a way of inserting itself into our consciousness as we write. It masquerades in its familiarity as what we "know" and "feel." It incessantly offers its words as "suitable" for the rhymes, or for the text in tow. Keep on the lookout to avoid these if you are writing serious or literary poems.

Using this "sensory" Goldberg strategy for identifying what I can creatively approach, and the reverse rhyming strategy you have just practiced to find out where the poem itself wants to go to find coherence, I am often surprised. I look up and see that three or four hours have slipped by me unawares. I have no idea where the time went. I am so stiff I can hardly stand. And I have a poem which astonishes me by having brought me out in a *new* and most often pleasant, sunny place. To borrow from Wallace Stevens, it is for me, for that day, "The Poem That Took the Place of a Mountain."

# 9. Reflections to Go — and Bon Voyage

Wallace Stevens, in *The Necessary Angel,* speaks of the nature of the truth that the poet recognizes by not by reason primarily but by *sensation.*

This speaks to me. It seems to me this is what poetry is largely about. A philosophical treatise, for example, can give you a reasoned truth, but that's not the same thing at all as a poetic truth. A poetic truth, drawing on the five senses, sings with vibrant music, juxtaposing images that make a tapestry of sensation you never quite felt before, yet one you recognize. You can't describe it to others except in the language of the poem. On subsequent readings it may be subtly different, larger, and deeper. Other individuals will hear a slightly different music, see different images, and feel their own lives reflected in a different manner, in each instance unique to themselves.

The powers of sensation that create poetic truth interest me deeply. I think of them as inherent in one's Mother Tongue. From *in utero* the unborn child is listening to its mother's heartbeat, her gurgling digestion, her voice resonating down from the voice box through the lungs and gut and into the embryonic sac. The soon-to-be-born baby experiences when the utterances of words correspond to the hormone-juices of truth, and when they do not. After its birth, as a child at her knees, it will more distantly confirm, nonverbally, their truth and falsity.

I think the poet's calling is to be as truthful to feeling as he or she possibly can be. In hewing to the "Ur-sensation" of *language as felt* (Mother Tongue, not the clichés of Madison Avenue), the poet lives it anew and revitalizes it for all of us.

*To live it anew and revitalize it for others,* even those in the human community one doesn't know personally, is a privilege.

Quite a privilege, don't you think?

In my heart of hearts I hope that the energies which formal poetry can release (as it has since before Shakespeare) might in some small way help shape in the 21$^{st}$ Century a less violent and more reflective social consciousness for the better.

These energies can bring to both poet and reader new awareness and mindfulness of a sustainable world of relationships, and of the truths which necessarily underlie them that we westerners seem increasingly today to ignore. If we reward readers sufficiently in poetry, it may move them to read more of it, and help shape a new consensus for involvement in the human community and natural world.

Most *non*-poetry readers complain that reading poetry is too much effort. Yet many of these, perhaps most, when questioned closely will admit that if they stumble accidently on poetry in magazines and public places and take time to read it, it's not all that bad. Some poems give them a smile or a laugh. Some increase their mindfulness of human nature and the natural world around them. Some poems contribute to their understanding of the complexities of people generally, and of their own unique relationships as well.

What makes poetry "too much effort," I submit, is the lack of reward for readers — a *pleasing artistry* which, too often today, poets *neglect* to put into their work. There's little to please the ear or the eye, or the craving for sophisticated rhythm comparable to that which draws youngsters and oldsters alike to concerts, symphonies, jazz, and rock. Readers will gladly expend effort if adequately rewarded.

It's true that good free verse employs (as does, of course, formal poetry) alliteration, assonance, and consonance. These furnish the poem with lyric notes. Rhetorical repetition offers foreground rhythm. But there is no background rhythm without meter and structural corner posts flagged with ear-pleasing end-rhymes to mark the turning of lines. Both are rhythmic drivers which entrain the brain. Without them, the *contrapuntal pleasure of speech stress is absent.* There is much less reward for the reader or listener.

Indeed, what is the reward for the *poet* who writes with less music than is available? Poets of non-rhyming, non-metrical work cannot experience the full underlying *incantatory power* found in formal ear-pleasing work. "Free" verse offers poets less reward *as art* on subliminal and subconscious levels. Without this reward, what can be in it for the poet as composer? For the reader? Or for the ever-shrinking numbers of people in the listening audience who today are entertained as much — or perhaps more — by the poet's physical "performance" as by the poetry?

How long will poetry last if "broken-prose MFA poets," as some call them, write and "perform" primarily for each other? Not long, I think.

Who is responsible? I think we poets are.

What do *you* think? What role will *you* play in the present and future times of poetry?

Thank you for inviting me to spend this time with you — and Bon Voyage!

# 10. References for Advanced Study

**Gwynn, R.S.** (Editor), *New Expansive Poetry,* Story Line Press, Ashland, OR, 1999. (An interesting group of broadly-ranging essays regarding the contemporary scene in formal poetry.)

**Kinzie, Mary,** *A Poet's Guide to Poetry,* The University of Chicago Press, Chicago, IL, 1999. (A comprehensive handbook of examples, principles, exercises, and terminology that will take you deep into the heart of formal poetry in all its variety of expression.)

**Steele, Timothy,** *All the Fun's in How You Say a Thing: An Explanation of Meter and Versification,* Ohio University Press, Athens, OH, 1999. (He's right. When you finish this volume, you will probably agree, as I certainly do, that's where all the fun is — as Robert Frost promised.)

**Steele, Timothy,** *Missing Measures: Modern Poetry and the Revolt Against Meter*, University of Arkansas Press, Fayetteville & London, 1990. (This is a closely studied, detailed history of metrical poetry's uses and abuses leading up to and including the revolt against it represented by William Carlos Williams and so many others.)

**Young, Sue,** *The New Comprehensive American Rhyming Dictionary,* Avon Books, NY, NY, 1991. (You'll find this a tremendously handy paperback volume containing over 65,000 entries of contemporary American English — including some clichéd and slang expressions best used only in humorous verse. It utilizes a key to spoken sounds that becomes increasingly familiar and easy to use for the serious poet-to-be who wants true ear-rhymes.)

On a limited budget? Buy Young's *Rhyming Dictionary* now. Borrow from your library, or by Inter-Library Loan, Steele's *All the Fun...* and Kinzie's *A Poet's Guide...*, in that order. Work with each until you are satisfied it is worth it to you personally to buy them. They will lead you to other resources.

**Your Notes:**

Made in the USA
Charleston, SC
08 September 2012